30 DAYS TO EMOTIONAL WELLNESS

DB BEDFORD

No part of this book may be reproduced, scanned, or distributed in any printed or electronic form without permission. Please do not participate in or encourage piracy of copyrighted materials in violation of the author's rights.

30 DAYS TO EMOTIONAL WELLNESS
Copyright © 2022 by Derrick DB Bedford
ALL RIGHTS RESERVED

ISBN - 9798420383858

Cover Design: Horseplay Studios/Stacey Debono
Edited by Stacey Debono

For more information, contact us at

www.ineverworry.com
db.bedford@ineverworry.com

TABLE OF CONTENTS

INTRODUCTION	9
MESSAGE FROM STEVE BACON	13
FOREWORD BY MINISTER MIGNON SEALS	17
DAY 1: EMOTIONAL WILLPOWER	21
DAY 2: EMOTIONAL CAPACITY	27
DAY 3: EMOTIONAL BIASES	33
DAY 4: EMOTIONAL BAGGAGE	39
DAY 5: EMOTIONAL GRUDGES	45
DAY 6: EMOTIONAL EQUATIONS	51
DAY 7: EMOTIONAL REBOOT	57
DAY 8: EMOTIONAL FITNESS	63
DAY 9: EMOTIONAL BURNOUT	69
DAY 10: EMOTIONAL RECHARGE	75
DAY 11: EMOTIONAL BALANCE	81
DAY 12: EMOTIONAL PROCESSING	87
DAY 13: EMOTIONAL FREQUENCY	93
DAY 14: EMOTIONAL BOUNDARIES	99
DAY 15: REVIEW	105
DAY 16: EMOTIONAL MATURITY	111
DAY 17: EMOTIONAL SEASONS	117
DAY 18: EMOTIONAL PARENTING	121
DAY 19: EMOTIONAL SPENDING	127
DAY 20: EMOTIONAL DISTRACTIONS	133
DAY 21: EMOTIONAL BEAST	139
DAY 22: EMOTIONAL REACTIVITY	147
DAY 23: EMOTIONAL CURRENCY	153
DAY 24: LAW OF OPPOSITES	157

DAY 25: EMOTIONAL FIRST RESPONDER	161
DAY 26: REVIEW	165
DAY 27: REVIEW	173
DAY 28: REVIEW	181
DAY 29: REVIEW	189
DAY 30: CONGRATULATIONS!	193
ABOUT THE AUTHOR	197

INTRODUCTION

I take my hat off to you for picking up this book and starting this 30 day journey because we all need to be honest about the impact emotions have on our day-to-day lives. Emotionally charged situations can show up very quickly. If you're not viewing your life through the lens of emotional intelligence, you're going to get caught off guard every single time. The things you say and do and how you react when something is emotionally charged can be very sensitive, and we can find ourselves in a space where we have to come back and do some damage control.

A wise man once said, "He who flies off in a rage never has a safe landing." If you act rashly in reaction to something that someone said to you, and you start telling yourself a story about why an injustice was done to you, it's going to disrupt your energy every single time. You're going to lose your focus from your peace at that moment.

This book was designed to minimize those low-frequency situations and ensure successful communication and relationships on all levels and every situation. Of course, it's not always going to be easy, and there are going to be times when you may miss the mark, but if you are committed to this emotional intelligence platform, you will begin to recognize how to bounce back quickly and effectively and stay on track. The harder we fall, the higher we bounce back, and the more you feel empowered to resolve those challenging situations through the lens of emotional intelligence, the stronger and more successful you're going to be. The people around you will start to notice it as well, and they're going to be craving that knowledge you possess. You're going to become a credible messenger of peace in your social circle *because emotional intelligence is contagious.*

You have just made a great decision to begin living your life through the lens of emotional intelligence. This is how it works: every day, you should strive to read a chapter that reveals a new EI skill, then focus on that skill for the following twenty-four hours. Consciously think about that skill: write it down, put it into the notepad of your cell phone, and read it throughout the day, whatever you need to do, just consciously and deeply think about that skill of the day. Stay focused and be true and honest with yourself with the questions at the end of the chapters. This is for *your* benefit and a gift you're giving yourself. At the same time, don't worry if you miss a day or two. It's easy to jump back in and get back on track.

It's also important to note that you can read from front to back, back to front, or start at any relevant chapter you desire. This is your journey. Do it at your pace. The important thing is that you get what you need out of it, that you are practicing the lessons, and bettering yourself.

Let's get started

PS – We also offer an online course and an audiobook version. Simply scan the QR code below for more information. Many employers offer reimbursement for these courses, so be sure to check with your HR Department. Either way, it's an excellent investment in your success – at work and home!

MESSAGE

Congratulations on committing to becoming even more emotionally intelligent! This is huge because when you look at the top income earners in corporate America, emotional intelligence is a large piece of all of that.

I'm Steve Bacon, founder and CEO of Belief Theory, and I'd like to briefly explain how your belief system is directly connected to emotional intelligence.

Your beliefs control your thoughts, your thoughts control your emotions, your emotions control your actions, your actions create your results, and your results reaffirm your beliefs. When I say your belief system is directly connected to your emotional intelligence, understand that *belief* is a strong emotion, not a fact. A belief is a strong emotion, a strong feeling. It doesn't mean that it's a fact. It may be true for you, but that doesn't mean it's true in the broader sense.

When it comes to emotional intelligence, understand that your emotions aren't just there for whatever reason. Your emotions have a purpose, and that purpose is like signals in a car. They tell you which direction you need to go or what you need to pay attention to. It's not about what the other person did; it's your reaction to it.

Let me give an example. The emotion of anger signals the brain that your core values have been violated. However, if you don't understand your core values, you'll have a tough time dissecting that emotion and how that feels.

Let me give you another example. If you yelled at me and I got angry, I have to understand a thought has triggered that anger, and that thought is being triggered by a belief I have, and that belief comes from a value that I have.

If I get angry because you yelled at me, I have to step aside and think, okay, why am I angry? One of my core values has been violated. Now we need to identify it. *Talk to me like an adult instead of yelling at me.*

If I feel violated because of someone's tone, then because of emotional intelligence and what DB teaches us, I know I need to sit, analyze that emotion, and think *What is the thought behind my feelings here?* I'm angry, but what is the thought? This person is disrespecting me by yelling at me. Now that thought is being led by a belief. If I'm being disrespected, what is my belief? The thought is I'm being talked to like a child. The belief is that I need to be respected as the man I am. Okay, great. Now that I have identified all of that, I can then figure out what I want to do with it because if this person talks to me a certain way, and then I get angry, but I don't analyze that emotion, I'm liable to pop off. I then find myself in trouble playing the victim for an emotion that I *chose* to feel based on my thoughts and beliefs.

It's important to understand that whenever you feel any emotion, whether it's anger, sadness, fear, hurt, guilt, each one of these emotions has a definition that allows you to trace back to the thought that created the emotion and the belief. If you master this understanding of how your beliefs are connected to your emotions, I promise you will be able to live life even-keeled and not take things personally because you understand why you feel that way.

Again, congratulations on choosing to participate in the *EI 30 Days of Wellness*. I'm so excited for you because you are on your way to a whole new level. Take care, God bless, and we'll see you over the top.

FORE WORD

There's *always* a way to live life better. The struggle for most people is not knowing there is a better way but discovering *how* to get there. Sheer desire is not enough. Information is necessary. Tools are necessary. And a consistent support system is necessary to obtain and maintain any degree of successful change. DB Bedford's *30 Days to Emotional Wellness* program is just that. He has created a system to help people live free, whole lives. He's removed every barrier, every plausible excuse, and has created a palatable, relatable, and most importantly, a doable program. This book provides participants with the requisite tools to meet the demands of daily life and live a life overflowing with balance, peace, and true internal happiness.

No matter your station in life, this book can help you. Whether you're investing in yourself as an individual or you're a corporation seeking to invest in its employees, the benefit is not unilateral. No one, no company which actively participates and puts in the work will remain unchanged. Lives and workplaces will be forever impacted.

I've spent more than 20 years of my life actively serving in ministry, and I retired from the healthcare industry to launch out into the world of "wellness" through entrepreneurism because I witnessed firsthand, in both contexts, the gaping void and great need for a program such as this. When DB launched *30 Days to Emotional Wellness*, I did not know that I, someone who has built a life and career around educating and supporting others on their journey to wellness, would personally benefit from it. Within a year and a half, I lost my grandmother, mother, my son's father, and my best friend. All of those losses within such a short time knocked the wind out of me. I have walked many people through crises, prepared them for death, and helped them rebound from tragedy. However, the healer must sometimes be poured into and undergirded during difficult seasons. My rebound, or emotional reboot, required a small investment of time each day. DB's program dulled the blows from the losses and diminished their impact on my life. I was back to my baseline by the time the program was over!

You don't have to become a byproduct of your experiences, nor do they have to shade or dictate the direction of your life. With each new day, we receive new chances and new choices. Every day we must make a concerted decision to live that day with the same degree of focus, strength, endurance, and INTENTIONALITY as the previous day. But if we're honest with ourselves, life can be downright fatiguing, and it doesn't take a crisis for that fatigue to occur. The *30 Days to Emotional Wellness* program will shore you up and provide you with the internal fortitude required to maintain that momentum for the rest of your life. All you have to do is put the information into practice.

If you are reading this foreword, you've taken a chance AND made a wise choice. You are in good hands with DB! This book is a life-changer! I am excited for you because this is the first day of the rest of your life. Squeeze every bit of good out of this book that you possibly can; take full advantage of your new emotional wellness and create the life you both desire and deserve!

Minister Mignon Seals / Chef Ming
Phase 8 Wellness
phase8wellness.com

"We are what we repeatedly do. Excellence, then, is not an act, but a habit." Aristotle

Emotional Willpower

This first day is significant because today, we start laying the foundation so that you can be successful and get the most out of the next thirty days. The important thing I want you to remember here is to make sure that you embrace these EI skills and brand them into your spirit so that you are ready to use them at a moment's notice.

For the next thirty days, I'm going to theme everything with "emotional" because we're talking about emotional intelligence and emotional wellness, and we want to keep that present. I will give you multiple ways to look at emotional intelligence and how to maintain emotional wellness from here on out. Today's particular strategy is what we like to call **emotional willpower**.

Please think about that for a second because **emotional willpower** is *critical*.

❖ What is **emotional willpower**?

It's the ability to override an unwanted thought, feeling, or impulse. This is when you feel like responding to someone who negatively comes at you, or you feel like sending that email when someone has pushed your buttons. I think we've all been there when you want to "go there." **Emotional willpower** will give you the strength to not "go there" impulsively. Just because you *can*, doesn't mean you *should*.

We want to make sure that we give ourselves a fair opportunity to be the best version of ourselves every day. It's really about taking the appropriate action at the moment, even when you don't feel like it. Not having emotional willpower can be damaging, not only to our careers but also to our relationships and our mental health. It's toxic energy. You can be around someone or in an environment you don't like, which can emotionally charge you, making you forget that you need to be practicing and have **emotional willpower**.

One of the ways to exercise and practice **emotional willpower** is to take a *purposeful pause*. This is when you intentionally put some space between your responses, especially to something negative. This space can be just a few seconds, but it gives you a chance to think about your response before impulsively reacting. Have you ever said something that you've instantly regretted? These purposeful pauses can help you think about how, or even IF, you're going to respond and hopefully eliminate those "regrettable" responses.

We like to say when you take a purposeful pause, you're giving logic time to catch up with you.

♞♜ Strategy of the Day

Think about **emotional willpower**, what it is, how it can benefit you, and sit with that for a few minutes. Pay attention to situations that may come up in the next 24 hours and see if you have the ability to resist any attitudes or negative moods that you may typically have by practicing **emotional willpower**. Observe those around you and see if you can notice it in others.

"Strength does not come from physical capacity. It comes from an indomitable will." Mahatma Gandhi

QUESTIONS

Think about what your defensible mental space may feel like. It could be just a brief pause in your thoughts or even a conscious thought to take a deep breath before you act or speak that gives you the space not to overreact and the ability to respond with emotional intelligence.

How would taking a pause before you act or speak help you in a situation?

_____
_____
_____
_____
_____
_____
_____
_____
_____
_____
_____
_____
_____
_____

How differently might a situation or conversation turn out had you not taken a purposeful pause?

_____
_____
_____
_____
_____
_____
_____
_____
_____
_____
_____
_____
_____
_____

Emotional Capacity

How did you do with your emotional willpower? Did you notice any conversations that may have given you the urge to be negative, to be a little aggressive? Were you able to resist those? Many things can annoy us in our daily lives. Maybe your kids got on your nerves, or your significant other or a co-worker said something slick. How did you do with your emotional willpower? Did you notice anyone else practicing it?

Sometimes we can feel a bit overwhelmed, so today we're talking about **emotional capacity.**

❖ What is **emotional capacity**?

Emotional capacity is our daily individual capacity for energy. Many of us get irritated or exhausted throughout the day because we don't understand that we each have a limited energy supply. You only can take so much for the day, and if you're aware that you only have so much energy budgeted for the next twenty-four hours, then you'll be mindful of who you give your energy to.

❖ How is having **emotional capacity** a benefit to us?

If your car had a full tank of gas, you still couldn't drive 1,000 miles without having to refill your tank, so even when you wake up and you're feeling your best, you still know you only have so much energy for the day. However, many of us *don't* wake up with a "full tank of gas" because we are still carrying things from the day before. Being mindful of your energy level is an excellent strategy for emotional wellness. Without enough "gas" or energy, we can't deal with things that come our way in an emotionally intelligent way. We might fly off the handle, and we might impulsively react to something without using a purposeful pause. This can result in hurt feelings, damaged relationships, or to the extreme, a loss of employment or worse.

❖ How do you protect your **emotional capacity**?

A great way to be mindful of your **emotional capacity** is to understand that you only have so much energy to spend each day. Have you ever had a "check engine light" come on in your car? For many of us, as long as our car starts, we still get in the car and keep going. However, that light is there for a reason. It's there to tell you that something is wrong, and we all know it's usually much more costly the longer you wait, and you risk the car completely breaking down.

It's the same with our energy. I believe we all have our own 'check engine' lights. They turn on when we're irritated or frustrated or when we seem to be in a bad mood for no reason. This is another indicator that our **emotional capacity** is getting low. Why is this important? Because if you step into the day on that low vibration with low energy and you're already irritable, it's going to have a direct impact on how you make decisions, how you deliver information, and how you process information.

It's essential to recharge your energy as well. Self-care is an integral part of recharging your energy. Meditating, physical exercise, reading, getting a manicure/pedicure, or doing something you love all contribute to positive mental health and go a long way towards refilling your gas tank. Try to avoid negative people and situations and stay away from negative energy, as this is a sure way to drain your capacity. These situations at times are unavoidable but remember that it's how you deal with them and how much energy you spend on them that is important. Be mindful of what you watch and listen to and the conversations you engage in.

Strategy of the Day

Think about **emotional capacity** and what it means to only have so much energy for the day. Monitor your energy levels for the next 24 hours, pay attention to those around you and see if you can get an idea of how much energy they are operating off of. Take five minutes for yourself to just breathe and refill your energy tank with positive thoughts.

"Atoms are driven by consciousness. In proximity to love, they move in harmonious collaboration with other atoms. When in proximity to fear, they become disharmonious and chaotic. We choose each moment the energy that surrounds us." Marianne Williamson

QUESTIONS

Pay attention to your patience level today and the emotions behind it. Did you reach your emotional capacity?

Think of a time you may have taken rash action in an emotional moment. How differently might things have turned out had you been patient had you let things work themselves out?

_____
_____
_____
_____
_____
_____
_____
_____
_____
_____
_____
_____

What EI skills could you utilize to protect your emotional capacity?

_____
_____
_____
_____
_____
_____
_____
_____

In what ways does protecting your emotional capacity benefit you personally?

_____
_____
_____
_____
_____
_____

03

Emotional Biases

By now, you should be starting to feel where we're going with these very simple and impactful nuggets. So far, we have talked about *emotional willpower* and resisting those negative urges. We talked about your *emotional capacity*; when you get up every single day, you only have so much energy to spend in a day. Today we want to talk about **emotional biases.**

❖ What are **emotional biases**?

We all have biases where we essentially see things only from our perspective. We want things to be the way we want them to be. I define these biases as **emotional biases** because we have a strong feeling behind them.

I want to tell you about three particular biases that you should look out for on a day-to-day basis. This first is *projection bias*. Your projection bias is usually activated when you see something you don't like and want to speak on it, and you wonder why it's a struggle for you to use your willpower. You have a strong belief about it, so you project your biases onto the next person. When you see somebody do something that you wouldn't do, or you hear somebody say something that you wouldn't say, it automatically gives you inner conflict. You're ready to respond. You're ready to react. This is where that emotional willpower comes in.

But pay attention to that projection bias. When we're practicing emotional intelligence, remember that as soon as something rubs you the wrong way, we need to stop looking at it from the perspective of, "This person made me mad," or "This situation rubs me the wrong way." Start asking yourself, "Why does that bother me in the first place?" Take a purposeful pause and reflect on that.

The second bias is *confirmation bias*. This is when you take a particular situation that happens to you and you reach out to people you know so that you can tell them what you just went through because you know they're probably going to side with you. You want to talk to someone who is more than likely going to agree with you. However, what if you were wrong in that situation? What if there was something you could have improved? If someone you trust and respect validates your wrong actions, then you're probably not going to be able to see any opportunities to improve. We all need to hear from different people, but make sure that you're not going to your cousin who always sides with you no matter what. You want to make sure you have people on your team who will help you see new perspectives. This is how we grow.

The last one is your *status quo bias*. If you do not like things to change and you need everything to be the way it's always been, and the minute something changes, you start to feel a certain kind of way. Why? Because you would prefer that it not change. You would prefer no flexibility or adjustment to the "status quo."

Imagine you've been using XYZ Insurance Carrier for 20 years. They provide coverage for your home and car. Your parents have used them for years as well, and you've never had any issues. They're a bit expensive, but they are reliable, so why should you switch? A trusted business associate has approached you with a money-saving alternative with an equally reliable company. Still, you refuse to listen to what they're saying because you've "had this company for years, there's no reason to change."

Now, had you taken a purposeful pause and put aside that status quo bias, you might have seen that the insurance policy not only saved you hundreds of dollars a year, but that policy was richer in benefits. How many opportunities have you passed up because of a status quo bias?

♞♜ Strategy of the Day

Keeping these biases in mind will allow you to rethink or reimagine a situation you're approaching to get the best results possible. Think about these biases within yourself and see if you can observe those in yourself and others. Spend the next twenty-four hours reevaluating yourself and your emotional biases. Be completely honest with yourself. You don't have to change your mind about these mindsets, only how you deal with them.

"Self-serving biases and self-centered agendas are cotton jammed in the ears of our conscience. Even if truth shouts, we cannot hear it." Craig D. Lounsbrough

QUESTIONS

What are some things you might be biased about?

___

How might those biases hinder your personal growth and emotional intelligence?

___

What steps are you willing to take to work through these biases so that you can grow?

___

Emotional Baggage

We're moving right along, and you should be starting to feel a little bit more connected to the mindset of emotional intelligence.

If you're taking the time to think through the Strategies of the Day, taking each of these skills and sitting with them throughout your day, and observing other people and what they're doing, it'll help you be mindful of being emotionally intelligent. They say it takes 21 – 30 days for a habit to form. I'll tell you one of my little secrets: If you're doing the Strategy of the Day every day, by the time we get to the 30th day, practicing emotional intelligence just might become a habit of yours, too. The first domain of emotional intelligence is Self-Awareness, so if you are aware of EI most of the time, you increase your chances of practicing it. We're doing it one day at a time to give you time to sit with what I'm sharing with you.

Today we're going to talk about **emotional baggage**.

❖ What is **emotional baggage**?

You may have heard Erykah Badu sing about something similar in her song, *Bag Lady*. "Bag lady, you goin' hurt your back, draggin' all them bags like that." We tend to bring all of our **emotional baggage**, past experiences, and past traumas that we have a habit of carrying into the present moment. After a while, those bags can get pretty heavy. They become a burden and slow us down.

Imagine going on a trip, and you have several pieces of luggage. You are not moving as quickly as you would if you just had one carry-on, right? To move fluidly, you have to pack light. This means every day you have to get into the habit of unpacking stuff that happened yesterday because once yesterday is over, it's over. Once words have been spoken, they've already been said. Whatever is done is done.

So many of us get hung up on what has happened that we lose sight of figuring out what to do next. We have no control over the past, only *the now*. I want you to be mindful of any **emotional baggage** you might be carrying. As I said, it could be from past life experiences. It could be from past relationships. It could be from poor decisions that you made in the past that are weighing you down. Get in the practice of packing light. I want you to practice this little simple thing I like to call "catch and release." Think about people who fish for sport. They catch a fish, they might take pictures with it, and then they throw it back. Catch and release. If negative things come your way, you can catch them, process them, but then release them. You want to do this to enable yourself to *pack light*. You want to be able to move more fluidly through life without having so much stuff weighing on you on a day-to-day basis.

If you make a mistake at work, don't agonize over it. Acknowledge it, learn from it, so you don't make that mistake again, and move on.

If someone hurts your feelings, discuss it with them in an emotionally intelligent way, decide which way to move based on that discussion, and move on. Harboring resentment only creates baggage, and again, the purpose here is to pack light. Release that resentment.

A wise old man once said, "You will never be able to fly if you don't give up the things that weigh you down." Keep that saying in mind when you think about this strategy of keeping your emotional baggage light, and you feel like things are getting heavy.

 Strategy of the Day

For the next 24 hours, check your baggage. Are you carrying things that you have no business carrying? You could probably let go of things that you could have processed by now.

Pay attention to those around you. When people's bags are heavy, their mood is low. They always have an attitude, or they have an attitude for no reason. This means there's probably some baggage that needs to be unpacked.

Think about **emotional baggage**, what it is, what kind of impact it can have on you, and why it's important to empty it for your emotional wellness.

"When I let go of what I am, I become what I might be." Lao Tzu

QUESTIONS

What steps did you take today to unpack your emotional baggage?

_____
_____
_____
_____
_____
_____

How did it feel once you took those steps?

_____
_____
_____
_____
_____

What are the benefits of not carrying all that baggage, and what will you do going forward to ensure that you "pack light"?

_____
_____
_____
_____
_____
_____
_____
_____
_____
_____
_____
_____
_____

Emotional Grudges

How are you doing? Is this stuff resonating with you? Is it making sense? Today, we're going to talk about **emotional grudges**.

❖ What is an **emotional grudge**?

I call them **emotional grudges** because we tend to be in our feelings when somebody does something that we don't like. Think about these **emotional grudges** because they are directly connected to your baggage.

It may be because of projection bias when you can't find it in your spirit and heart to let something go. That grudge is so strong because it hit one of our personal beliefs. Remember, projection bias is when you've projected onto this person, and it's upsetting you because that may not be what *you* would've personally done or said.

Someone once said, "Holding a grudge or resentment towards someone is like taking poison yourself and expecting the other person to die." What does that mean? Why might you have this feeling about someone or a situation? Often, they're not even thinking about you/the situation, and may not even know you have a grudge against them. That's all the more reason why you need to let that grudge go.

The next thing I want you to do is forgive, but remember, forgive for *you*, not for them. However, forgiving doesn't mean forgetting; I want to clarify that. I also want to remind you about harboring resentment and baggage. Catch and release, right? We can *forgive* for ourselves and our own mental health because that clears up emotional baggage. We don't have to *forget* the situation, but that doesn't necessarily mean we have to harbor resentment either because that takes up energy and creates unnecessary baggage.

Taking things personally is the fastest way to hold a grudge and the fastest way to build anger. It can also be the fastest way to disappointment. Understand that everyone is operating from their own set of internal software, so if it feels like it's personal, more often than not, this isn't the case.

Internal software is a combination of your beliefs, values, and life experiences. Everybody's operating from a different perspective. If you practice not taking things personally, even when it *feels* like it's personal, you will get better at not holding grudges. Often, people who have not done the work you're doing right now don't know how to communicate or articulate their emotions or feelings. They don't know how to process things. You are in a special place because you're learning how to flow through that and not hold these energy-draining emotional grudges.

Strategy of the Day

For the next 24 hours, if you have any grudges, it's time to unpack them and throw them out with that excess emotional baggage. If you know anyone who's holding a grudge, suggest that they try not to take things personally. Encourage them to forgive, but not to forget. If that doesn't work, tell them what the wise old man said: *"Holding a grudge or being angry at somebody is like taking poison yourself and expecting the other person to die."* You're the only one feeling the pain while the other person is off living their life. Being angry poisons *your* energy, holding on to grudges weighs down *your* baggage, and taking things personally fuels negativity.

"Carrying a grudge is difficult work that brings nothing of value. Forgive, and be free." Ralph Marston

QUES TIONS

Think about any grudges you might have right now and consciously tell yourself, "I will let them go." How does this make you feel?

_____
_____
_____
_____
_____
_____
_____
_____
_____
_____
_____
_____
_____

How can avoiding holding grudges in the future benefit your emotional intelligence?

_____
_____
_____
_____
_____
_____
_____
_____
_____
_____
_____
_____
_____
_____
_____
_____

06

Emotional Equations

Have you released those emotional grudges yet? I know that was a heavy one, and sometimes it takes a little longer to get through some of these practices; trust me, I get it. However, don't be discouraged if you feel like it's taking a while to work through a lot of this stuff; it took me a while, too. I promise you, though, if you go through the process and make it through the whole 30 days, you won't even know why you were holding onto those grudges in the first place.

Now, let's talk about something I like to call **emotional equations**.

❖ What are **emotional equations**?

Emotional equations are simplified solutions to everyday problems. They are quick nuggets that you can think about when it's time to process something happening in front of you.

The first equation is **S + R = O**, or ***Situations plus your Response equals an Outcome***. Situations are going to happen. You may not have any control over a situation, but you *do* control how you respond to that situation. Your emotional willpower comes into play here when you feel like responding to a situation in a negative way, so it's imperative to be aware and take those purposeful pauses. *Your response is directly related to the outcome.* Often, we can change the entire direction of an entire situation just by our response. We have the power to fuel the fire or diffuse tension, all in our response. This is a simple **emotional equation** to think about every time a situation arises.

Another equation is **E + E = P** or ***Emotions + Emotions usually equals a Problem***. If two people are emotional over a situation, this usually turns into a problem because they are not thinking logically. This more than likely happens when the people involved in the situation have not exercised emotional willpower and purposeful pauses, and the situation has escalated. Remember the first equation once you realize this has happened: S + R = O. You can still control your responses and use logic instead of emotions.

This is important to keep that in mind and dovetails into the following equation: **E + L = S**, or ***Emotions plus Logic usually equals a Solution.***

When you're emotional, and the person you are talking to is emotional, there's a good chance the situation will end up in a problem, so keep in mind that you will want to replace those emotions with logic. When you can engage in this situation from a logical lens, you are utilizing one of the emotional intelligence strategies.

♞♜ Strategy of the Day

Take the next 24 hours and observe situations as they arise. Know that you don't have control over the situation, only your reaction. Be observant of your reaction and keep in mind that when emotions are high, logic is low.

"Success is the sum of small efforts, repeated day in and day out." Robert Collier

QUESTIONS

What types of emotions did you experience during your day, and how did you handle them?

_____
_____
_____
_____
_____
_____
_____

What did you observe when you handled a situation with logic versus emotion? How did you feel?

_____
_____
_____
_____
_____
_____
_____
_____
_____
_____
_____
_____
_____
_____
_____
_____
_____
_____
_____
_____
_____

07

Emotional Reboot

You are one week in, and I hope it went by smoothly. Now we want to talk about something we like to call an **emotional reboot**.

❖ What is an **emotional reboot**?

An **emotional reboot** is vital because, as you know, there are times throughout the day when people can get on your nerves. Maybe you see something that agitates you while you're at work or home, and you might need a quick way to recalibrate yourself. The **emotional reboot** is the ability to reset your energy in the heat of a negative experience. Keep this in mind because, while sometimes you try your best to prevent yourself from getting in a situation, you find yourself in them anyway. To keep those situations from escalating, this is when you want to initiate an **emotional reboot**.

If you've ever had to reboot your computer, there are three keys that you have to press – *ctrl, alt,* and *delete*. One of the reasons we would want to reboot is because sometimes the computer has a glitch or it's not functioning properly, or perhaps you might just need to give it a fresh start. I want you to take that same concept of "ctrl, alt, delete," but think about it from an emotional wellness standpoint.

"**Ctrl**" - *control yourself* in the situation or prevent yourself from escalating it.

"**Alt**" - *look for an alternative solution* or another perspective. Look for what could be done differently to increase the chances of a more positive outcome.

"**Delete**" - *remove yourself* from the situation because often, you can get clarity if you just step back and take a purposeful pause.

Strategy of the Day

This strategy is simple but powerful, but keep in mind that all of these things work individually or together; it just depends on the situation. With practice, you will discern which to use with no thought at all because it will become a habit.

Take the next 24 hours and pay special attention to your situations as they arise – perhaps there was a long line at the grocery store or a miscommunication with a coworker. Make a concerted effort to control your reactions. Look for alternative solutions to adverse problems. Remove yourself if necessary.

"There is virtue in work, and there is virtue in rest. Use both and overlook neither." Alan Cohen

QUESTIONS

In what positive ways could you control your emotions in an emotionally charged situation?

_____
_____
_____
_____
_____
_____

What might be some positive alternative solutions to negative situations?

_____
_____
_____
_____
_____
_____

How would removing yourself from a situation benefit a "heated argument"? What is the benefit to you? What is the benefit to the situation? How might the "heated argument" have been prevented in the first place?

_____
_____
_____
_____
_____
_____
_____
_____
_____
_____
_____

08

Emotional Fitness

We've been together for about a week now, and you've had an opportunity to marinate each day on these EI skills. We've touched on these different strategies for you to practice emotional intelligence and embrace emotional wellness. You're building your EI muscles!

What we're going to talk about today is **emotional fitness**.

❖ What is **emotional fitness**?

Typically, when we talk about *fitness*, we're referring to working out and keeping ourselves in shape physically. When it comes to **emotional fitness**, it's the same thing but from a mental standpoint.

We want to *intentionally* practice emotional intelligence every day and pay attention to the results. So that means that every day, which is what you've been doing for the last week, you are keeping EI fresh in your mind. However, you want to put some intention behind it. You consciously know that this is what you're doing, and this will help you grow and get stronger, just like you know if you work out or exercise, you'll get physically stronger. If you constantly work on your emotional intelligence, you're improving your emotional wellness. We're going to do that through **emotional fitness**.

A key way to improve your EI fitness is to be *intentional*. Read something every day on emotional intelligence. It could be specifically about emotional intelligence, or it could be a story in news where people have lost control through their emotions, and you think about what could have been done differently from an emotional intelligence lens. These are both excellent ways to exercise your emotional wellness muscles. Keeping EI as a conscious thought helps keep it as an intentional action.

♞♜ Strategy of the Day

Pay attention to the emotions of others. Be like a kid on a playground looking at all the different activities going on but pay attention to what other people are doing and how they're handling things. That's the real-life practice of emotional intelligence, seeing who can do it and who isn't doing it so well.

And lastly, reverse engineer your days and your conversations. This means simply looking back, seeing what went well and what didn't go so well. We want to keep doing the things that went well because we got good results. We either want to adjust the things that didn't go so well or stop doing them. These are all surefire ways to improve your EI fitness.

"Do not let the things that try to steal your peace rob you of your joy. Do not give them the permission to scare you into no performance." Precious Avwunuma Emodamori

QUESTIONS

Read a news headline and discern how it relates to emotional intelligence. Did someone use emotional intelligence in the way they handled a particular situation? If so, how?

_____
_____
_____
_____
_____
_____
_____
_____
_____
_____
_____
_____
_____
_____

If not, how could they have used emotional intelligence to better that particular situation?

_____
_____
_____
_____
_____
_____
_____
_____
_____
_____
_____
_____
_____
_____
_____
_____
_____

09

Emotional Burnout

Today's topic is about something we all want to be very mindful of, especially in our fast-paced lives, and that's **emotional burnout**.

❖ What is **emotional burnout**?

Emotional burnout simply refers to when you've had enough. You may feel overly exhausted, overworked, overextended, and underappreciated. These things will cause **emotional burnout**.

One of the ways you can avoid **emotional burnout** is to avoid racing against time. Have you ever seen someone on the road zoom right past you, then you catch up with them at the next light? They were going nowhere fast, right? Sometimes, we do the same thing throughout the day with our own deadlines and timelines. We feel like we have to do this, we have to do that. We are constantly trying to race against time. However, we have to slow down a little bit and understand that *we only can do what we can do*. This is very, very important.

Your inbox will always be full. We have to stop feeling like we have to get through those emails, answer every text, take every phone call right now. There will always be another phone call, another text, another email. Try to manage yourself appropriately and give yourself a break. Allow yourself to move with the flow.

Often, we have this mentality about grinding when trying to reach our goals. I used to have that mentality, too. But, when you think about it, what does that mean logically? Grinding means that you're going to wear something down until it's no more. When you're grinding and hustling and working and overextending yourself, you are setting yourself up for an **emotional burnout**.

Remember to control or handle only what you can. Don't worry about what you cannot. This is one of the simple but powerful strategies to avoid **emotional burnout**. Avoid taking on too much and feeling like you need to take over the world. You don't have to be everything for everybody. You don't have to take on other people's problems, and you don't have to "set yourself on fire to keep other people warm." Keep that in mind today, and ask yourself, "Am I emotionally burned out? Does everything feel heavy?" You'll know if the burnout is there and when it's time to do something to unpack that.

Strategy of the Day

Take the next 24 hours and pay attention to yourself and those around you. And remember, don't race against time. Control what you can and make a concerted effort to not worry about what you can't. Stress is usually activated when your expectations don't match reality. A lot of times in life, it is what it is.

"If you feel burnout setting in, if you feel demoralized and exhausted, it is best, for the sake of everyone, to withdraw and restore yourself." Dalai Lama

QUESTIONS

Think about some things you've been stressed about recently, perhaps some things you're stressing about right now.

What are you stressing about right now? What emotions are attached to that stress?

_____
_____
_____
_____
_____
_____

How do stress and emotional burnout hinder emotional intelligence?

_____
_____
_____
_____
_____
_____
_____
_____
_____
_____
_____

What can you do to avoid emotional burnout right now?

_____
_____
_____
_____
_____
_____
_____
_____

Emotional Recharge

You're a third of the way there, and it's super cool that you keep showing up. This means you are serious, and a big shout out to you for the commitment because it's hard for us to stay committed and consistent these days with all of the things going on in the world.

We talked about emotional burnout and emotional baggage and things of that nature, now I want to talk about **emotional recharge**. We want to keep this in mind to make sure that we recharge our mental batteries.

❖ What is an **emotional recharge**?

What happens when your cell phone battery starts getting low? The first thing you do is start looking for a charger. Before you leave the house on a trip, you make sure you have a charger. We keep those cell phones charged up. Most people are very intentional in ensuring that their batteries are charged because we want to ensure that they operate when needed. So, if you intend on making sure that your cell phone battery is charged, why not make sure your mental battery is charged the same way?

How do you keep yourself recharged? Well, there are a couple of strategies I like to use. One, I like to *"go dark"* at least once a day, every day. I take at least 15 minutes where I do absolutely nothing. I don't look at my phone, and I don't talk to anyone. You don't have to meditate, but you can. It's a good time to detach yourself from all the information coming at you and just be still and allow your body to recalibrate itself. I like to go dark for at least 15 minutes. Sometimes I'll go longer, but it's vital to detach and try to do nothing, by myself, and be still. It helps minimize that emotional burnout we talked about on Day 9.

Another strategy is to practice *sleep hygiene*. Sleep hygiene is not about sleeping or how many hours you get each night. It's more about your sleep quality because you can sleep for several hours and wake up still tired. Often, when we go to bed, we're going to bed with our heavy baggage on our minds. We might go to bed with the TV on, or we're scrolling through our phones, and all that stuff is sitting on our minds as we fall asleep. Then we're tossing and turning all night, which affects our sleep quality. Perhaps there are medical issues that might prevent you from getting a good night's sleep. Sleep hygiene is more about *preparing* to go to sleep, not just about the act of *falling* asleep.

Good sleep hygiene is scheduling your sleep, knowing what time you're going to bed, and creating a positive and conducive environment in which to do so. Make sure the lights are turned off. Studies show that you should disconnect from the TV and the phone at least an hour before you go to bed. Make sure your room temperature is cool to get a good quality sleep.

The other part of it is what we like to call *shower therapy*. This is the concept of imagining as you're washing away the dirt and the germs of the day, you're also washing away any problems, negativity, and bad energy. You're visualizing any negativity leaving you and going down the drain, just like the dirt that you're washing away.

Strategy of the Day

Practice these three strategies, as they are great ways to recharge yourself. Go dark once a day; take a break. Make sure you're sleeping correctly and that you have some good sleep hygiene. And then last but not least, practice some good shower therapy and wake up fresh in the morning, ready to face the day. Don't touch your phone as soon as you get up in the morning. Give yourself time to wake up before you start taking in information. This will help recharge that mental battery on a day-to-day basis.

During the middle of the day, perhaps during a lunch break, take that little *go dark* time. Every chance you get, just like when you plug your phone in to charge its battery, take the time to put that same energy into a mental recharge for yourself.

"Each person deserves a day away in which no problems are confronted, no solutions searched for. Each of us needs to withdraw from cares which will not withdraw from us." Maya Angelou

QUESTIONS

How do you think keeping yourself emotionally recharged helps you in your relationships and work-life?

_____
_____
_____
_____
_____
_____

Are you practicing healthy sleep habits? If so, list them. If not, what changes and commitments will you make to ensure you are?

_____
_____
_____
_____
_____
_____
_____
_____
_____
_____
_____
_____
_____
_____
_____
_____
_____
_____
_____
_____

11
Emotional Balance

Today, we'll talk about something I like to call the **emotional balance**.

❖ What is the **emotional balance**?

Emotional intelligence is really about keeping our emotions balanced. The simplest way to do this is to understand that when *emotions are high, logic is low*.

The higher the emotion is in any situation, the lower the logic. Imagine a scale that's been tipped because of an emotional situation. Whenever you find yourself emotional or see someone else being emotional, you have to either try to do something to bring the emotions down or just allow the emotions to subside to allow that scale to get back to a balanced position.

Most people tend to forget that you can't stay mad forever. You have to come down sometime, and the same goes for the other person – they have to come down too. Most of the time, we get triggered by their high emotions, and that's why it seems like the anger or "fight" goes on forever. The same goes true on the other side of the spectrum. We rarely stay excited or super happy before something happens to get us down for one reason or another.

It's an excellent practice to wake up every single day, no matter what's happening, and definitively decide on not getting too excited about any one thing *or* too down on another. You want to keep an emotionally even balance. Keep those scales on an even keel. Again, when emotions are high, logic is low.

Now, I'm not saying that you can never get super happy. Of course, we want to enjoy life when life is good. And because life is life, sometimes things can get heavy, but for us not to stay there in that space, for us not to let that impact the next thing that we have to do, we know that things have to balance at the end of the day. It may be off from time to time. Sometimes our logic may be super high, and the emotions will be low, or vice versa, but we know the sweet spot is when emotions and logic are pretty much in balance.

Strategy of the Day

For the next 24 hours, think about the type of person you are. Do you operate more out of logic or more out of emotion, or are you somewhere in the middle? Do you agree that the higher the emotions, the lower the logic is in certain situations?

"Balance is the key to everything. What we do, think, say, eat, feel, they all require awareness and through this awareness we can grow." Koi Fresco

QUESTIONS

In what ways could you create emotional balance in your life?

What could you do to balance your mood if you find yourself starting to have a bad day?

What emotional intelligence skills are essential to maintaining a healthy balance, and why?

Emotional Processing

We are almost to our halfway point. Today's topic is **emotional processing.**

❖ What is **emotional processing**?

When we talk about our internal software, or our beliefs, values, and life experiences, keep in mind that when people are giving you information, or when you read or hear something, you are processing that through your internal software. We call it **emotional processing** because your beliefs come with strong feelings, your values come with strong feelings, and your past experiences come with strong feelings. Depending on what you believe and value and what you've been through in the past will determine how you process things. **Emotional processing** is this idea of understanding *how* you process things emotionally.

We talked on Day 11 about emotional balance. Are you processing things from a logical lens, or do you process things from an emotional lens? That's going to have a lot to do with how you were raised. Were you allowed to express yourself when you were growing up, or were you not allowed to process your feelings? Depending on where you are with that is going to have a determination on how you are processing. Sometimes, you will find that others can't process what you're telling them if you say just the slightest thing to them. They get into their feelings right away and are immediately very defensive. We talked about grudges and not taking things personally. That's where a lot of that comes from. **Emotional processing** is necessary because it's understanding and being honest about how you process things.

♞ Strategy of the Day

Are you processing life through an emotional or logical lens or your past experiences? Are things bucking up against your belief system? Is your belief system outdated? How can you upgrade your internal software?

These are the things that we want you to work on and consider. Think about your **emotional processing**. Next time somebody says something to you, be mindful of the first thing you want to respond, defend, or engage with. Will you be calm enough to listen? Take a new perspective and understand where they're coming from.

"To master your emotions is not to suppress them. It is to process them with diligence and express them with intelligence." Kam Taj

QUESTIONS

Today, practice not taking things personally. Think about whether you are someone who takes things personally. Can you make that adjustment? Trust me; if you can embrace this one, you will free yourself and move a lot lighter in any situation.

Think about something that happened today that you might have taken personally. How might you have turned that around and not taken it personally?

___

How does not taking things personally further your emotional intelligence?

___

Can you process things logically versus emotionally?

___

13

Emotional Frequency

Emotional frequency, one of my favorites. Either someone is vibrating on a low frequency, or they're vibrating on a higher frequency.

❖ What is an **emotional frequency**?

In this platform, we describe low-frequency people as those who always tend to be negative. They've got a problem for every solution. We want to practice minimizing our time with them, if not avoiding them at all, because they will lower your vibration.

High-frequency individuals, those of us practicing emotional intelligence, have a high level of emotional wellness. High-frequency individuals look for positivity. We're solution-oriented. We understand that *it is what it is*, even though it may not always be what we'd like it to be. We don't have time for negativity. We don't have time for the people telling us what we can't do. We've all got a family member or a friend who's always bringing you bad news, sad news, downer news, right? We don't want that in our lives.

Part of your emotional wellness is making sure you vibrate at a higher frequency. When you see people vibrating low, the best thing to do is vibrate higher when you see that negativity. What does that mean? It's just how it sounds. They say eagles don't soar with pigeons. You want to fly at your highest altitude and be at your best as much as possible.

When people are vibrating at a low frequency, and if they can't receive what you're saying to try to change their mood, then the first thing that you do is gracefully bow out. You want to move on. You should only seek and connect with people vibrating on your same frequency.

What frequency are you on? Do you feel like you vibrate on a low frequency or a higher frequency most of the time? Emotional frequency is about the energy that we emote on a day-to-day basis. Energy cannot be created or destroyed. It just exists, and you know energy exists because you can feel it when people come into your presence. Energy, both positive and negative, can be transferred from person to person without us even realizing it. This is why it's essential to be at our best at all times and be around high-frequency people as much as possible.

Strategy of the Day

Think about the emotional vibrations in your life. Think about how you've been feeling today and in the past few days. Think about the other people around you. For the next twenty-four hours, check your emotional vibrations. Are you vibrating high? Are you vibrating low? Are you vibrating somewhere in the middle? Any one of them is okay. What you do with them is where the intelligent part comes in.

"I've learned that people will forget what you said, people will forget what you did, but people will never forget how you made them feel." Maya Angelou

QUESTIONS

How did people around you react when you were vibrating high? Low? What about when you were somewhere in the middle?

_____
_____
_____
_____
_____
_____
_____
_____
_____
_____
_____
_____
_____
_____
_____
_____
_____
_____
_____

What are some things you could do to bring up your mood when you feel low?

_____
_____
_____
_____
_____
_____
_____
_____
_____
_____
_____
_____

14

Emotional Boundaries

Today's topic is about protecting your peace with **emotional boundaries**.

Let's sit with this one for a second.

❖ What are **emotional boundaries**?

We've been talking a lot about ourselves, but this one has a lot to do with other people. I just want you to make sure that you are protecting your peace at all times. This piggybacks on emotional frequencies. We don't have time for low frequencies, and part of that is understanding that we need to protect our peace because you can't have peace of mind if you always have to give people a piece of your mind, right?

You've got to find that emotional balance. If you don't draw the line, people will always cross it. You have to set your boundaries: what you will and will not engage in. It doesn't have to be a loud announcement; you just utilize your skills, recognize who you should engage with, and who you should give some space to. We'll talk more about that in the next chapter but remember, if you never draw the line in life, people will always cross it.

You might be one of those personality types who always wants to help others. However, just because somebody throws you the ball doesn't mean you always have to catch it. Just because somebody throws you a conversation, or somebody tries to reel you in, doesn't mean you have to engage. There is a saying, "When things are going wrong, it doesn't mean that you have to go with them." When people are trying to throw their situations at you, try to remember you don't have to catch it, you can let that ball go out of bounds.

My favorite saying when it comes to emotional boundaries that I like to tell people is, *"Stop setting yourself on fire trying to keep other people warm."* That's a significant component of emotional wellness. What does that mean? If it makes you uncomfortable, but it makes them comfortable, it's probably something that you shouldn't be doing. There's nothing wrong with self-preservation. There's nothing wrong with taking care of yourself first. They tell you on the airplane that if the flight happens to go sideways, put your oxygen mask on first, then you can help others. After all, if you don't take care of yourself effectively, how can you do the same for others?

Strategy of the Day

Where are your **emotional boundaries**? I want you to ask yourself, "Am I setting myself on fire just to keep other people warm? Am I catching every ball coming my way?" Have you not drawn a line? These are good self-reflecting questions to sit with. Practice respectfully drawing those lines, finding that emotional balance, so that you can protect your peace.

"You have to be able to set boundaries, otherwise the rest of the world is telling you who you are and what you should be doing. You can still be a nice person and set boundaries." Oprah Winfrey

QUESTIONS

Do you feel you have boundaries in your life? If so, how do you maintain those boundaries? If not, what steps do you need to take to set up sustaining boundaries?

_____
_____
_____
_____
_____
_____
_____
_____
_____
_____
_____
_____
_____
_____
_____
_____
_____
_____
_____
_____

Why are boundaries vital to emotional intelligence?

_____
_____
_____
_____
_____
_____
_____
_____
_____
_____
_____
_____
_____

Review

We are halfway through, and this is an excellent opportunity to review the fundamentals of emotional intelligence. This is very important because there's so much to take in that we sometimes forget about the fundamentals. We need to make sure that we are operating from these fundamentals every day regarding our emotional intelligence and our level of emotional wellness.

The four fundamentals of emotional intelligence are *self-awareness, managing your reactions, situational awareness,* and *relationship management*.

Simply put, *self-awareness* is always being mindful of your mood, attitude, and the energy you bring to any situation.

Managing your reactions is being responsible for how you act, no matter how you feel. We already know we have no control over what happens to us. We *do* have control over how we respond.

Situational awareness is the quick assessment of whether you should engage. Should I engage with this person, or should I give them some space? It's a rapid internal assessment. You assess the situation and determine whether it is low vibrating, or negative. If the emotions are too high, then you simply back off to protect your peace.

Relationship management is putting a lot of value on your relationships and nurturing and managing them so that everyone involved is vibrating at a higher level so that you can live a fulfilling life.

Remember, self-awareness and your ability to manage your reactions are what we call your *personal competencies* and have everything to do with *you*. Self-awareness is number one because this all starts with you no matter what. Remember, you have to invest time for this to work so that you have a high level of emotional intelligence and can be emotionally well. You have to spend more time looking in the mirror instead of looking out the window. What does that mean? Stop looking at what everybody else is doing and critiquing everybody else and take that same energy and apply it to yourself. Situational awareness and managing the relationships around you are what we call your *social competencies*, and that has to do with *others*.

QUESTIONS

What are the four fundamentals of emotional intelligence?

_____
_____
_____
_____

What does *self-awareness* mean to you?

_____
_____
_____

What does *managing your reactions* mean to you?

_____
_____
_____

What does *situational awareness* mean to you?

_____
_____
_____

What does *relationship management* mean to you?

_____
_____
_____

Self-awareness and managing your reactions are _____ competencies.

Situational and managing the relationships around you are _____ competencies.

"Smile, and let everyone know that today, you're a lot stronger than you were yesterday." Drake

16

Emotional Maturity

How are you feeling about being self-aware, being mindful of how you respond to things? Are you using situational awareness, deciding whether certain energy is energy you should engage in, or if it's energy you should give some space to?

On Day 15, we talked about relationship management, and it's important to note that people with positive vibes are our greatest resource. They add value to our emotional wellness while we're practicing emotional intelligence. Today we'll talk about **emotional maturity**.

❖ What is **emotional maturity**?

We know that age doesn't necessarily come with maturity. It's the same thing with our emotions. You have to be mindful of how far you've come and if you've grown in this space. I'm sure there was a time in your life when challenging situations happened, things irritated you, and you responded one particular way. You know that you have moved forward with your **emotional maturity** when you don't respond that same way. There's a saying, *"The things I used to trip off of, I just walk over now."* This is a display of **emotional maturity**. Ask yourself where you are regarding how you process challenging situations, irritating situations, and being around people you don't like. Is it all in your face these days, or are you able to hold your head high and have a poker face? Just because you *can* say something, you don't always *need* to say something. Can you reserve how you feel about something and then let it out on the other side? That is a display of **emotional maturity**. The core thing I want you to remember is that you're always responsible for how you act, no matter how you feel.

♞♜ <u>Strategy of the Day</u>

Emotional maturity is the challenge for the day. Identify any areas in your life where you might feel like you may be overreacting to the little things, where you're not viewing things through the lens of emotional intelligence. For the next twenty-four hours, think about **emotional maturity**. Pay attention to situations and start the process of not having the desire to be right. This doesn't mean you're wrong! It just means you're not right to the *other* person or the situation. It's about keeping an open mind in every situation and seeking to understand instead of seeking right or wrong.

"We can't solve our problems with the same thinking we used when we created them."
Albert Einstein

QUESTIONS

Was there a situation today where you had to be right? Could you have let it go and just accepted someone else's perspective?

_____
_____
_____
_____
_____
_____
_____

How might accepting another perspective be good for our emotional intelligence?

_____
_____
_____
_____
_____
_____
_____
_____

How does not having the desire to be right play into emotional intelligence?

_____
_____
_____
_____
_____
_____
_____
_____
_____

17

Emotional Seasons

Today I want to introduce you to something that helps me accept that I will not stay in whatever mood I happen to be in. I like to call this the **emotional seasons**.

❖ What are the **emotional seasons**?

We know that the seasons will change, so if I connect that to your emotions, you know that you don't stay mad or happy, just like it never stays summer or winter. Our emotions are constantly changing depending on the circumstances around us. I think about these **emotional seasons** whenever I find myself in a tight squeeze or when things are not going right. I consider my bad times my winter season because winter is usually cold, rainy, and somewhat dark. And again, I know that winter will not stay around forever. Eventually, winter turns into spring, and brighter days are ahead. I'm vibing on that higher frequency again and feeling new and fresh, a time for growth. And then that may turn into longer, warmer days, your summer. We know summer turns into fall, the time for reinventing yourself, spending time with family, relationship management.

Unfortunately, our moods are not predictable like the seasons. However, if we recognize them as they come, take a purposeful pause, manage our reactions, and manage our emotional balances, these moods can be easier to weather. **Emotional seasons** are something that can help you understand that change is inevitable. Even when things are feeling good, understand that the next season might be coming so you can stay prepared.

♜ Strategy of the Day

For the next twenty-four hours, check yourself so you don't wreck yourself, as the saying goes. Then after you take a look in the mirror at your own attitude, pay attention to the attitudes of others. The world of emotional intelligence is like one big learning ground, and we're paying attention to others for the purpose of learning. Not to critique, not to judge or gossip, but to learn what to embrace, what could be done better and how we can optimize our performance every day, in every area of our life.

QUESTIONS

How was your mood throughout the day? Did you experience many mood changes?

_____
_____
_____

If you experienced some lows in your attitude, what did you do to bring yourself back up? Would you do anything differently next time?

_____
_____
_____
_____
_____
_____
_____
_____
_____
_____
_____

Did you notice any mood changes in others? If so, what changed their mood? Do you think anything *could* have changed their mood?

_____
_____
_____
_____
_____
_____
_____
_____

18
Emotional Parenting

Today we're going to talk about **emotional parenting**. This can apply whether you are a parent, are going to become a parent, or know someone who is.

❖ What is **emotional parenting**?

We've talked about your beliefs, values, and life experiences, which come from whoever had guardianship over you as a child. This dictates in large part how you raise your own children. There's a study that shows that there are two different types of parenting styles: The first is what we call the *emotional dismisser*. Being raised as a young male in East Oakland was rough. I'd take a walk to the store, and I would be surrounded by dudes who would either take my bike or Starter jacket, then I'd run back to the house, scared. But my father would tell me, "Boy, you better get back out there and fight!" If I felt sad or cried about something when I was young, my parents would tell me, "You better hush your mouth before I give something to cry about." These are examples of emotional dismissers. I never had the opportunity to feel my emotions to even understand them. What happens when you keep those emotions packed down? You don't really know or learn how to respond to things appropriately.

The second type of parenting style is an *emotional coach*. This is the parent who allows their child to feel their emotions, no matter what they are, and they help them manage those emotions instead of dismissing them.

This is no pot shot at our parents because they did the best they could. But if you're an emotional dismisser and you never give your child an opportunity to express themselves, and you're telling them to do something because you said so, you're not providing them a space to communicate their feelings or emotions appropriately. They will keep those emotions bottled up, only to surface later in life and often in negative ways.

♟♜ **Strategy of the Day**

This is about sitting with yourself for a little bit, and there's no right or wrong, but it's good to identify how you were raised and how it affects you now. Are you carrying baggage? Is it time to update your internal software in this area?

If you're a parent, think about how you were raised and how if affects parenting your own children.

"Always be nice to your children because they are the ones who will choose your rest home." Phillis Diller

QUESTIONS

If you are a parent, are/were you an emotional dismisser or an emotional coach?

_____
_____
_____

What type of parents did you have? How you were raised has a lot to do with how you are processing emotions today.

_____
_____
_____

How could you use emotional intelligence to temper your responses when your children might set you off?

_____
_____
_____
_____
_____
_____
_____

In what ways could setting the example of using emotional intelligence benefit your children now and in the future?

_____
_____
_____
_____
_____
_____
_____
_____

19

Emotional Spending

Let's talk about emotions and money. The **emotional spending** segment is a bird's-eye view of what type of spender you are, and it also goes back to your beliefs around money.

❖ What is **emotional spending**?

Were you raised in a space where money was considered a scarcity? Were you told, "Money doesn't grow on trees!" or "Waste not, want not!"? When you think about your beliefs around money, that also comes from how you were raised. There are different ways we look at money, but you want to consider the personality you developed around money.

At this point, you may have already been introduced to the different EI personality styles. To tie those into **emotional spending** and how you spend money, you might be a Gold Personality Style if you are a person who is very structured around money. You're an avid saver, you set up budgets, you know where every dollar is going, and you might be considered a "penny pincher."

Do you like to plan and budget? If you are a Green Personality Style, you're very analytical and do a lot of research before spending. If you need to buy something from Best Buy, you might look at a few other electronic stores to see who has the best deal. You're more of a researcher, slightly different from the Gold Personality, who plans out how to spend their money.

If you are a Blue Personality Style, you spend money a little bit more freely. You're the person who might be out shopping for yourself, and then you'll see something and think, "Oh, my friend could use this," or "This person would appreciate that." Blues tend to lead with their heart and think about how to spend money on other people.

The Orange Personality is the spontaneous spender, the risk-taker. They are more likely to take risks with their investments. If they are at Best Buy, they are likely to be more impulsive, grabbing stuff off the shelves and throwing it in the cart. There is less regard for price comparisons than Green or Gold Personality Styles.

Strategy of the Day

Understanding which type of spender you might be can also be leveraged and used in terms of how you want to grow your money. If you prefer to plan everything out, you might miss life-changing opportunities that don't go with those plans. Alternatively, always jumping on every opportunity regardless of risk might have an impact on you in the long run. It's just something to think about when we talk about **emotional spending**. If you look at your portfolio, your bank accounts, and your spending habits, and you are trying to get a handle on how you can do better, it's not always about, "Let me cut off this subscription or that extravagance." You can also take a deeper dive and say, "What kind of spender am I?" Do I look at the price of things before I spend, or does that not matter at all? Do I shop and compare? Am I always spending my money on somebody else? There are a lot of different ways to think about it.

"Be not afraid of growing slowly, be afraid only of standing still." Chinese proverb

QUESTIONS

What kind of spender are you? Are you a structured spender, an analytical spender, a spontaneous spender, or are you someone who splurges on everybody else?

How does the type of spender you are help and hinder your emotional intelligence?

Emotional Distractions

We're in the home stretch now! Good job for staying committed.

I want to talk to you today about **emotional distractions**.

❖ What are **emotional distractions**?

Emotional distractions can happen both internally and externally. Some of your external **emotional distractions** are social media, radio, or TV, and the negativity you encounter through people and conversations. They're going to happen in the workplace, when you're out running errands, or even in traffic on the freeway. These external places are all places where someone might try to pull your energy.

I call it a distraction because the goal, remember, is to get up every single day and have the best day ever. Most of us get up with the intention to at least have a *good* day, but then something happens, and it distracts us from that. These are **emotional distractions** because there's a feeling behind getting knocked off track. Be mindful of what you're looking at on social media, what you're listening to, who you're engaging with when you go out, and how people are interacting with you; don't let these distractions hijack your emotions.

Then there are the internal distractions. This might happen when you're not feeling well. Maybe you didn't get enough rest, or you're hungry, or both, and that will have an impact on how you process information, how you deliver information, and how you're feeling when engaging with people.

You want to be aware. Remember, the first domain is self-awareness, and you want to be aware of potential **emotional distractions** so that you're not derailed from the ultimate goal of having the best day ever.

Don't bite the hook if people are trying to engage you in negativity. Think about a fish in the water minding his own business, and a fisherman comes along and throws his line in the water. The fish could ignore the line if it didn't have bait on it, but the bait becomes irresistible, so he jumps on the bait only to get snatched out of his environment, never to return. There'll be hooks of negativity dancing around your environment all day, ready to distract you. You have to remember that it will lower your vibration if you bite that hook. It's going to lower your frequency and take you out of your positive environment, change your mood, and change your attitude. That's what we're trying to avoid.

You don't have to stop at every barking dog. If you stop at every barking dog or at every little thing that's vying for your attention, it takes you longer to get to your destination. And in some cases, you might never reach it in the first place. **Emotional distractions** are essential to recognize in your wellness program because they will keep you from the goal, which is to be positive. Optimize your day, have the best day ever, because this day right here is the only day that we actually have.

Strategy of the Day

Today's challenge is to think about what might be emotionally distracting you. Are those distractions worth losing your focus on the goal that you're trying to achieve? More than likely, these things have emotional connections for you. Find a way to focus on your goals and things that bring you positivity.

"Starve your distractions, feed your focus."
Anonymous

QUESTIONS

What are some of the things you were distracted by today?

_____
_____
_____
_____
_____
_____

How can you refocus yourself when you find yourself distracted?

_____
_____
_____
_____
_____
_____

How can being distracted hinder your emotional intelligence?

_____
_____
_____
_____
_____
_____

Listen to other people in your life. What are some of the things that they may be emotionally distracted by?

_____
_____
_____
_____

21

Emotional Beast

Now, I know these skills are simple, but don't let that fool you into thinking that makes them any less effective. I break these down into such a simple form so that you can remember them when you need them the most. And there are several of them so that you can find that right combination as you see fit on a day-to-day basis.

This one right here is always in my emotional intelligence skill rotation and is about your **emotional beast**.

❖ What is an **emotional beast**?

We all have an angry beast inside of us, and, for the most part, that beast is in hibernation. Think about a time when you've been really, really angry, and you just lost it. You might have said whatever was on your mind, perhaps slammed doors, maybe even threw an object or two. You didn't even think about it – you were going to do what you were going to do, and whatever was in the way was not a concern at that moment. You didn't see it – or care for that matter – at the time because that **emotional beast** was *angry*. The emotional beast had been let loose, and it was running rampant. That's why I call it a beast because when that anger rises, it is super hard to bring them back down.

It's essential to be mindful of your **emotional beast**. You will want to keep yours at rest at all times. Think about a giant beast escaping from its cage at the zoo and attacking people. There is not much that bystanders can do because that beast is usually bigger and stronger than humans; it's ferocious and stronger. It's going to tear up whatever is in its path, and then whenever it calms down, the only thing that's left is destruction. If you could put that in perspective when you get angry, whether your beast is in full rage mode or even stands up a little bit and growls and bites and snaps at someone, once the beast in you calms back down, then you're left to clean up the casualties and the mess that it made. You'll have to apologize for any hurt feelings, miscommunications, repair ruined relationships, or worse, mourn lost relationships.

In all of my years of living, I've never thought to myself after my beast has come out and calmed down, "I'm proud of you, boy." I've regretted the destruction that beast has caused, whether it was my fault or not. We regret those casualties, the estranged relationships, the damaged property, whatever results from our anger. Missed opportunities, estranged relationships, or toxic work and family environments can also happen.

You can see how many of the skills you've already learned are not only stand-alone lessons but also go together hand in hand. For example, you learn to control your emotional beast with emotional maturity and self-awareness. As situations that might trigger that emotional beast occur, take that purposeful pause...step away from those negative emotional frequencies. And finally, know that this emotional season will pass, and sunnier days are just around the corner.

Strategy of the Day

I want you to be mindful of your **emotional beast**. Keep that in mind for the next 24 hours. Just think about your beast and think about other people's beasts that have come out and what happened as a result.

"If you are patient in one moment of anger, you will escape a hundred days of sorrow."
Chinese proverb

QUESTIONS

What happened when you let your emotional beast stand up? What was the result of unleashing that beast?

___

What happened when you saw the emotional beast come out in someone else? What kind of path of destruction did it create?

How different might the outcomes of those situations have been had you or the other person kept that emotional beast asleep? In what ways might you keep that beast quiet?

_____
_____
_____
_____
_____
_____
_____
_____
_____
_____
_____
_____
_____
_____
_____
_____
_____
_____

"A negative mind will never give you a positive life." Buddha

22

Emotional Reactivity

Today's lesson is about **emotional reactivity**.

❖ What is **emotional reactivity**?

Emotional reactivity is the level at which you react to things. We all know someone who puts the two on the ten, and the littlest thing that happens to them quickly elevates to a level ten right away. **Emotional reactivity** is understanding how you respond to things and how you react to things and keeping this in mind as you engage. When things happen, no matter how big or small, you have to ask yourself, "Am I remaining calm under pressure?" Or does almost everything just push your button, rub you the wrong way, and you get irritated right away?

Do you ever find yourself frequently saying, "I'm irritated!" or, "This gets on my nerves!" This is directly related to your **emotional reactivity**, the level at which you react or respond to things. This is very important because when you're practicing emotional intelligence, you want to get into a space where you are less reactive, regardless of what's happening, so that you can be in the mindset to move quickly to solutions. If you are always hot and you're always ready to clap back, and if you're quick to get an attitude, then that will stunt your growth a bit when it comes to emotional maturity.

 Strategy of the Day

What is your level of **emotional reactivity** on a scale of one to five? One means that you're always calm under pressure, three means you could go either way, and four and five means you "go there." Be honest with yourself.

Where should you be in life? Ideally, you should be three and under, and you really should be careful with the three because sometimes you just can't help yourself when something close to you is being impacted. Practice staying in that one and two, understanding that you don't control those situations when something happens. We only have control over *how* we respond. Remember, we talked about this in emotional equations.

For the next 24 hours, start thinking about what your mental defensible space may feel like. It could be just a brief pause in your thoughts or even a conscious thought to take a deep breath before you act or speak that gives you the space to not overreact, and the ability to respond with emotional intelligence.

"Life is 10% what happens to you, and 90% how you react to it." Unknown

QUESTIONS

How would taking a purposeful pause before you acted or spoke help you in a situation?

_____
_____
_____
_____
_____
_____
_____
_____
_____
_____
_____
_____
_____
_____
_____
_____
_____

How differently might that situation or conversation have turned out had you not taken that purposeful pause?

_____
_____
_____
_____
_____
_____
_____
_____
_____
_____
_____
_____
_____
_____

23

Emotional Currency

This particular EI skill ties into the fourth domain of emotional intelligence, the fundamental of managing relationships. Are people depositing good energy into you? Or do they just take energy away from you? This makes me think about how we spend money; either we make a deposit, or we make a withdrawal. When you are engaging with people, either you are pouring into people, or you're taking away from them. And in this life, we are put here to use each other, but we're not put here to *misuse* each other. This lesson is about **emotional currency**.

❖ What is **emotional currency**?

Many people miss the importance of having positive and solid relationships. I don't mean just knowing people. I'm referring to people feeling good about knowing you, when your name comes up, and they feel they're proud to say, "Oh, that's my friend!" It's a great feeling when others feel proud that they are friends with you. When people are happy to look out for you, that means that you have deposited good energy into their life. You've made more deposits than withdrawals. This helps make the world go around in a positive way. I'm one of those people who is proud to say that my **emotional currency** is in the black when it comes to wealth with energy.

♟♜ <u>Strategy of the Day</u>

If you can understand the power of intentionally making people feel good, you see the value in emotional wellness. It feels good to love people and when people love you right back. Think about your emotional currency right now. How are you spending it? Are you depositing it into people, or are you just taking it away? Wherever you're at, that's okay.

In this process, we're raising awareness and giving you things to reflect on. As you grow into this space, emotional currency is vital. It's so important to be good to people and having people you're connected to brings a higher vibration to your life. That way, you don't have to spend a lot of time protecting your peace because everyone around you brings peace.

QUESTIONS

What are you doing to foster solid relationships with people so that they feel good about knowing YOU?

_____
_____
_____
_____
_____
_____
_____
_____
_____
_____

List a few people you value in your circle as solid and positive relationships that you would consider "emotional currency."

_____
_____
_____
_____
_____
_____
_____
_____
_____
_____
_____
_____
_____
_____
_____
_____

Law of Opposites

Today's skill might be familiar to you, but I had to put it into the fold because it's important. I told you a couple of days ago about your emotional seasons and how seasons change. This will also strengthen that. Today we are going to talk about the **law of opposites**.

❖ What is the **law of opposites**?

The **law of opposites** suggests that if there's an inside, there's an outside. When things are up, they must come down.

This also means if there's good, there also has to be bad, and when things are bad, there has to be good. So how can this help you with emotional wellness and when you're practicing emotional intelligence? When you're thinking about your emotional wellness, think about this: when things are going badly, when sometimes things just get a little funky and you experience a little emotional turbulence, you have to believe that it's not going to stay that way. There's always a positive side to everything because of the **law of opposites**. Just like when things are going well, don't get too comfortable because something bad can happen at a moment's notice. It's always wise to be emotionally prepared for this. This also supports the emotional balance we talked about on Day 11. When something bad or good happens, you're going to feel it. We might feel an initial shock, but we don't want to stay there because you can quickly move into acceptance. Manage your reaction so that you can move to a solution.

Strategy of the Day

Life is a trip. One day you can be sitting at the table, and the next day you can be on the menu. When you keep that in perspective, you can accept life for what it is and not always what you think it should be. This helps you from overreacting to things. This helps you put things in perspective faster when you understand the **law of opposites**. There's good, there's bad, and there's an inside, there's outside. So no matter where you are, no matter what you're doing, always know that there's another way to look at whatever situation you're in.

QUESTIONS

What does the law of opposites mean to you as it relates to emotional intelligence?

_____

How does over (or under) reacting to things hinder our emotional intelligence?

_____

25

Emotional First Responder

I recently saw this phrase, and it made so much sense in the EI world. I want you to consider yourself an **emotional first responder**.

❖ What is an **emotional first responder**?

Just like firefighters, police officers, and medical personnel who are the first ones on the scene to provide help in an emergency, **emotional first responders** put their mind and spirit in a position to help first no matter what is happening. Let me put that in perspective.

When a fire breaks out, that's a heavy and tragic thing. Even if someone sets the fire intentionally, the firefighters don't show up trying to figure out *who* started the fire. They want to put the fire out, ensure everyone is safe, and take care of people. Once everyone is safe, they can then figure out how the fire started.

There are fiery conversations that come at you all the time. It can get hot real fast in the workplace, at home, in your relationships with your kids or your spouse, but instead of trying to figure out *how* it started, be in a position to help put those fires out, bring the emotions down first. Once you have that settled, you can figure out the source. And you *do* want to figure out the source, not so that you can punish, but so that you can understand how it started in the first place, and then help somebody or guide them in a way so that it doesn't happen again. The term, **emotional first responder**, puts you in the mindset to help first instead of reacting first.

Remember, when emotions are high, logic is low. Utilize all the skills you've learned – emotional equations (emotions + logic usually equals a solution), taking those important purposeful pauses, ctrl/alt/delete – and you will be armed as a successful emotional first responder. It's also important to remember to protect your peace. If the fire is too hot, step away and wait until things cool down.

♞♜ Strategy of the Day

For the next twenty-four hours, pay attention to any scenarios that might flare up. Can you help without reacting?

QUESTIONS

How does figuring out the source of the problem after things have calmed down help a situation?

___

How would you protect your peace as an emotional first responder?

___

How would you go about diffusing a "hot" situation at work? At home?

___

Review

Day 26, and it's time to do a brief review. The review is an opportunity to package up everything you've learned in the last 25 days and bundle them up. It's also another good way to use these strategies and refer to them as needed.

We started this off on Day 1 with **emotional willpower**, and willpower has everything to do with being able to resist the urge when you don't feel like practicing emotional intelligence, where you don't feel like being in a good mood. It was designed so that you have that inner drive to be emotionally intelligent and to tap into your emotional wellness as needed.

On Day 2, we talked about **emotional capacity**, knowing that when we step outside every single day, we only have so much energy and you have to use it wisely.

On Day 3, we went into **emotional biases**. *Projection bias* is understanding that whenever you are bothered or upset about something, instead of looking at the situation and thinking that someone may have rubbed you the wrong way or you're mad about something, we start asking ourselves, "Why does this even make me mad in the first place?"

Confirmation bias means that we usually go to people who will side with us. This usually stunts or prohibits our perspectives and growth. If there was something you could've improved on, you're going to miss the opportunity simply because your sidekick or your ride-or-die will agree with you. Even if they disagree with you, they're going to minimize the issue.

Then we rounded it off with the *status quo bias*. It's tough to see new perspectives if you don't like things to change.

On Day 4, we talked about **emotional baggage**, when we carry stuff from the past and let it weigh us down. We know emotional baggage is not good and can impact our staying in tune with our wellness and practicing emotional intelligence.

On Day 5, we talked about those **emotional grudges**. These occur when we have a conflict with somebody, or somebody does something we don't like, and we start to resent them. Holding a grudge is like taking poison yourself and expecting the other person to die.

On Day 6, we dove into **emotional equations**. These were some quick, simple solutions to common everyday problems. We talked about understanding that situations plus a response equals an outcome. When emotions stack on emotions, they usually come with problems, and we know the fastest way to a solution is emotions plus logic equals solutions.

We ended the week on Day 7 with the **emotional reboot**. When you find yourself in the middle of something, you know that the way to recalibrate quickly and get back on a positive note is to hit those three keys: *control, alt, and delete*. Control the situation, look for alternatives, and delete the toxic or negative feeling you're having by removing yourself from the situation.

"He has the most who is content with the least." Buddha

QUESTIONS

What does *emotional willpower* mean to you?

_____
_____
_____
_____
_____

What does *emotional capacity* mean to you?

_____
_____
_____
_____
_____

What are the three emotional biases, and what do they mean to you?

_____
_____
_____
_____
_____
_____
_____
_____
_____

What does *emotional baggage* mean to you?

_____
_____
_____
_____

What do *emotional grudges* mean to you?

_____
_____
_____
_____
_____

What do *emotional equations* mean to you?

_____
_____
_____
_____
_____

What does *emotional reboot* mean to you?

_____
_____
_____
_____
_____

"One of the secrets of success is to refuse to let temporary setbacks defeat us." Mary Kay Ash

27

Review

In week two, we talked about some critical things. On Day 8, we talked about **emotional fitness** when practicing emotional intelligence. When you build your body up for fitness, you have to go to the gym. You have to exercise your body to attain your fitness goals, and the same goes for emotional intelligence. If you want to be emotionally well to the point where it shows in your healthy relationships and successful life, I recommend that you read something about emotional intelligence and practice EI in your daily interactions, just like you've been doing for the last 25 plus days. By now, your fitness should be up. It's essential to keep going after this. That's the key.

On Day 9, we went over **emotional burnout**. If you ignore how you're engaging, what you're taking in, you risk getting emotionally burned out.

Day 11 was all about the **emotional recharge** and how to bounce back from that burnout. We need to be mindful of putting ourselves to bed at night and practicing good sleep hygiene. We talked about shower therapy and going dark for at least 15 minutes a day, where you're doing absolutely nothing in that time to reset yourself. You allow your energy to just sit for a second and not have to work at doing anything. It's almost like when people fast, right? You fast to give your digestive system time to process everything and just relax a little bit—same thing with the recharge. You want to give the energy in your body time to recover before you get back into life.

On Day 12, we talked about our **emotional balance**. Always remember the higher the emotion, the lower the logic. When you're engaging with people, you have to keep a balance within yourself every day. Ideally, you want to engage with people who also have that balance within themselves.

On Day 13, we discussed **emotional processing** and being mindful of how you feel when information is coming in. How do you feel about what you're hearing? As you start to take yourself through a step-by-step way to respond, you're mindful of how you feel about it. Emotional processing is essential.

Day 14 was about those **emotional frequencies**, the high frequencies (positive) and low frequencies (negative). You want to make sure you're on your highest frequency every single day. You want to be mindful and watch out for those who operate on a low frequency and avoid engaging in negative conversations or situations.

And finally, we rounded off week two on Day 15 with **emotional boundaries.** If people throw you the ball, you don't always have to catch it. I want you to remember this saying in particular: *Don't set yourself on fire to keep other people warm.*

"Don't judge each day by the harvest you reap, but by the seeds that you plant."
Robert Louis Stevenson

QUESTIONS

What does *emotional fitness* mean to you?

_____
_____
_____
_____
_____

What does *emotional burnout* mean to you?

_____
_____
_____
_____
_____

What does *emotional recharge* mean to you?

_____
_____
_____
_____
_____

What does *emotional balance* mean to you?

_____
_____
_____
_____
_____

What does *emotional processing* mean to you?

_____

_____
_____
_____
_____

What does *emotional frequency* mean to you?

_____
_____
_____
_____
_____

What do *emotional boundaries* mean to you?

_____
_____
_____
_____
_____

"Positive energy is attracted to positive energy." Deborah Day

28

Review

You should feel good at this point because you're just a couple of days away from finishing the 30 Day Emotional Wellness program. You now have the tools to protect your emotional wellness and apply emotional intelligence at a moment's notice. And better yet, you can also influence others to do the same.

Let's talk about what you picked up in Week 3. We went over the four domains of emotional intelligence. We talked about the fundamentals, *self-awareness,* and *managing your reactions*. Emotional intelligence broken down is emotions, how do I feel? And intelligence, what do I do with that feeling? Those are your *personal competencies*.

Then you learned *situational awareness* and *managing relationships*. Those were your *social competencies*. Situational awareness, making quick assessments, and thinking, "Is this energy I need to engage in or give space to? Is this a low vibrating conversation?" Always strive to vibrate higher and positively.

On Day 16, we talked about **emotional maturity**. Maturity doesn't automatically come with age. Your behavior dictates your maturity. You don't get emotionally mature without intentionally raising your emotions and learning how to process those regardless of what's happening around you.

On Day 17, we discussed **emotional seasons**, which was important because it reminded us that things change. This will help keep things in perspective when things don't go smoothly for you. When the days are cloudy, rest assured sunny days are ahead.

Then we brought it home on Day 18 and talked about **emotional parenting.** There are two types of parents – emotionally dismissive and emotional coaches. Emotionally dismissive parents don't provide their children with an opportunity to express their emotions or express themselves freely. They stifle their emotions, which results in the child bottling up those emotions, with little to no guidance or tools on how to process them effectively. This can lead to issues, such as emotional baggage, later on in life. The emotional coach is the exact opposite. This type of parent allows for the safe expression of emotion and allows the child to manage their feelings effectively. This provides an opportunity for emotional maturity. This is important when it comes to how we deal with emotions.

On Day 19, we hit you in the pockets with **emotional spending**. We took a quick look at what personality style governs how you spend money. We wanted to have a deeper understanding of how you view money and your beliefs around money. Money isn't everything, but when you don't have a handle on your finances, an understanding of where your money is going, or how to accumulate it and make more, it's going to impact how you show up.

On Day 20, we talked about those **emotional distractions** because the goal is to have a positive day every day. We don't want to get emotionally distracted. Remember that those distractions can come at us externally (social media, TV, conversations, etc.) and internally (your health, hunger, tiredness, etc.).

Then there was that **emotional beast** on Day 21. We don't ever want our beast to wake up, tear things up, strain relationships, and make decisions from which we can't bounce back. We discussed how important it is to exercise self-awareness, emotional maturity, utilize our purposeful pauses and protect our peace to keep that beast sound asleep.

"Energy is valuable. Spend yours where it's worthy." Unknown

QUESTIONS

What are the four domains of emotional intelligence?

___

What does *emotional maturity* mean to you?

___

What do the *emotional seasons* mean to you?

___

What does *emotional parenting* mean to you?

___

What does *emotional spending* mean to you?

___

What do *emotional distractions* mean to you?

What does *emotional beast* mean to you?

What do *emotional grudges* mean to you?

"The first step towards getting somewhere is to decide you're not going to stay where you are." JP Morgan

29

Review

Day 29, our last day of review!

We started Day 22 by talking about **emotional reactivity**. This falls under your personal competencies and is your awareness of how you react to things and then managing your reactions.

We then talked about **emotional currency** on Day 23. We touched on the social competencies, the energy that you exchange with the people that you come in contact with regularly. We equated it to making more deposits than withdrawals and understanding the value of those contacts. It doesn't matter if you're in contact with two people or 20 people, do your best to make people feel good about simply being connected to you.

On Day 24, we discussed the **law of opposites**. The law of opposites helps you put things in perspective. Remember, there are always two sides to every coin. How you feel today doesn't mean it's a permanent situation. If there's bad, there's good. The opposite is also true, so remember to keep that balance so you don't get caught off guard when trying to be the best version of yourself.

On Day 25, we talked about the **emotional first responder**. The emergency first responder's primary job is to help people, no matter who's to blame or who's at fault. When you're an emotional first responder, the first thing you should do is help people in a situation, even though they may have "started it." This can help you with your kids, your significant other, or even a difficult co-worker. Anytime you see someone do something or you're engaged in a situation where someone could have done better, diffusing that situation is being an emotional first responder. This can even include stepping away from the situation altogether if it becomes too hot.

QUESTIONS

What does *emotional reactivity* mean to you?

_____
_____
_____
_____
_____

What does *emotional currency* mean to you?

_____
_____
_____
_____
_____

What does *the law of opposites* mean to you?

_____
_____
_____
_____
_____

What does it mean to be an *emotional first responder* to you?

_____
_____
_____
_____
_____

Congratulations!

Congratulations! You just went through 30 days of taking in powerful, life-changing emotional intelligence skills. You've been processing them, reflecting on yourself, then taking a look at others and applying these skillsets to your daily life. How do you feel? You should feel good. It doesn't matter if you did the 30 days consecutively or if it took you 45 days. The point is that you did 30 days of embracing these emotional intelligence skills, which makes you more emotionally intelligent in every situation that you step into. That's something to be proud of.

Many people aren't aware of emotional intelligence yet, and if they are, very few can articulate what that means. Most people couldn't tell you the four domains of emotional intelligence, but you can: *self-awareness, managing your reactions, situational awareness,* and *managing relationships*. You understand that self-awareness and managing your reactions are the personal competencies in the process.

How do I feel? That's the emotion. What do you do with that feeling? That's the intelligence part. You've learned that the core fundamentals of being emotionally intelligent are the ability to process emotionally charged situations through a logical lens. We learned that the higher the emotion, the lower the logic.

How do you move forward now; where do you go from here? How do you show up and *be* emotionally intelligent? You're going to wake up every day and remember that you are responsible for how you act, no matter how you feel.

Once you acknowledge whoever you pray to, you should give thanks and have some gratitude. Gratitude is vital; we should all be grateful just for being alive. The easiest thing to do is remember that you are supposed to be operating from a centered space and peace, with your emotional balance intact. And how does that happen? It happens by taking time to keep your mental battery charged throughout the day.

You're also going to put some space between your responses. You're going to make sure that you don't start the day with expectations. You will stay emotionally prepared for people or situations that may switch up on you. You're going to travel light and stay baggage-free. So, when things happen to you throughout the day, you may process them emotionally, but when you learn to process things logically, you increase your chances of a positive outcome.

Emotional intelligence is the number one asset that employers will be looking for in the years to come, and you're already ahead of the game. You should be in a better space at home, with your family, co-workers, and friends. Remember, no matter what comes your way, from the extreme to the minute, the key is when you get up every day, you're looking at the world through this lens of emotional intelligence. It's like when you don't have your glasses, and the world is a little foggy; everything becomes clear once you put those glasses on. It's the same with viewing the world through the lens of emotional intelligence.

Be excited! Feel powerful! You've now got all these fancy emotional intelligence skills that have made you a better version of yourself.

Congratulations again; I'm so happy that you have completed this journey! Don't forget to share with your colleagues, family, and friends!

"He who returns from a journey is not the same as he who left." Chinese proverb

ABOUT THE AUTHOR

ABOUT THE AUTHOR

DB Bedford is a professional emotional intelligence consultant and has been consulting and training individuals, organizations, companies, and couples for close to 20 years. He has a strong passion for working with youth, families, and the community.

Being an inspiration to others and a role model to his children is of utmost importance. His goal is to leave a legacy behind so that 100 years from now, the world will know that he was here.

www.ineverworry.com

Made in the USA
Middletown, DE
17 April 2024